Ann and Liv Cross Antarctica

A Dream Come True!

By Zoë Alderfer Ryan • Illustrations by Nicholas Reti

Da Capo Press

A Member of the Perseus Books Group

Cataloging-in-Publication data for this book is available from the Library of Congress
First Da Capo Press edition 2003

ISBN 0-7382-0934-1

Published by Da Capo Press
A Member of the Perseus Books Group
www.dacapopress.com

Da Capo Press books are available at special discounts for bulk purchases in the U.S. by corporations, institutions, and other organizations. For more information, please contact the Special Markets Department at the Perseus Books Group, 11 Cambridge Center, Cambridge, MA 02142, or call (800)255-1514 or (617)252-5298, or e-mail j.mccrary@perseusbooks.com.

Set in 18-point Black Beard

1 2 3 4 5 6 7 8 9——06 05 04 03

To
Ann and Liv
Thanks for inspiring us!

DREAMING - THE MID 1960's

It all began as a dream.

Two young girls who lived on different continents had a dream. Inspired by past Antarctic explorers Ernest Shackleton, Roald Amundsen and Robert F. Scott, Ann Bancroft in Minnesota and Liv Arnesen in Norway, dreamt of one day crossing Antarctica.

"You are crazy!" said some.
Others cried, "You certainly will freeze!"
"Women can't go there!" the boldest declared.

But nothing, not even thoughtless words, could discourage them from thinking about the remote and fascinating continent. One day, as fate would have it, they met and soon discovered they shared the same dream - to cross Antarctica!

PLANNING 1998 - 2000

Ann and Liv decided that together they would work to achieve their dream. They began planning an expedition to cross Antarctica and the Bancroft Arnesen Expedition was born!

Two women - one dream!
To cross Antarctica from Queen Maud Land to the Ross Ice Shelf!
2,400 miles/3,840 kilometers in 100 days!
Pulling 250 pound/113 kilogram sleds!

Planning was the first step to achieving their dream - to cross Antarctica.

TRAINING 1998 - 2000

To get their bodies in shape for the long, grueling trip, they ran, they biked, they hiked and canoed. They even pulled tires attached to their waists because it was like pulling the sleds they would use in Antarctica.

Then they selected their equipment. They had to carefully choose all the right clothes to wear from their heads to their toes. Tents and sleeping bags had to be specially made. Sleds were constructed, skis were selected and sails were perfected.

The explorers also wanted to make sure the communications equipment that would keep them in touch with people around the world would stand up to Antarctica's extremely cold temperatures. The coldest place they could find to test it was in a very large ice cream freezer. So, between large boxes of frozen ice cream, they tried out their hand-held radios and practiced writing on their laptop computers.

After two years of training and planning, they were one step closer to achieving their dream - to cross Antarctica.

WORLDWIDE INVITATION

Ann and Liv wanted to share their dream with the world. So with the help of the Internet, they invited people from around the globe to "ride with them on their sleds."
Along came:

Students and teachers
Girl Scouts® and troop leaders
Parents and children
Grandparents and grandchildren and many more!

They all wanted to share in Ann and Liv's dream - to cross Antarctica!

THE DREAM BECOMES REALITY

Finally, with their planning and preparation complete, Ann and Liv were ready to begin!

They boarded a plane in South Africa and flew to Queen Maud Land on Antarctica. The plane landed and they stepped out into the freezing cold air. In the distance, mountain peaks rose sharply into the sky. Around them, blue ice stretched as far as their eyes could see. It was like a blanket spread over the continent's surface. They were in awe of Antarctica's magnificent beauty.

Ann and Liv had no time to waste. Antarctica's short 3 1/2 month "summer" is the only time of the year when it is light enough and "warm" enough to travel. The rest of the year it is so dark and cold it is impossible for anyone to survive outside.

Eagerly, Ann and Liv put on their skis and began to pull their sleds up the Sigyn Glacier and toward their dream - to cross Antarctica.

A DAY IN THE LIFE OF ANN AND LIV

Ann and Liv rose early each morning. Liv greeted the day by singing her heavily accented version of, "Oh, What a Beautiful Morning..." Ann, not being a morning person, awoke and her first thought was, "Cocoa!" Once they had wiped the sleep out of their eyes they began cooking their breakfast of cocoa and oatmeal. Then they melted ice so they could have water to drink for the day.

After breakfast the explorers packed up their sleds and carefully checked their equipment. Safety was their first priority.

Then off they went skiing and windsailing further and further across the frozen continent. They never stopped for lunch. Instead, every hour they stopped to snack on chocolate, dried fruit or nuts and lots of potato chips washed down with a sport drink full of vitamins and minerals.

Each evening, after a hard day's work, Ann and Liv stopped to make camp. Off went their skis and up went their tent. They warmed their cold bodies with a hot, freeze-dried meal of pasta, beef or fish.

After dinner they talked about their day and often read poetry to one another. This helped to take their minds off their sore muscles and tired bodies. They also wrote in their journals and repaired their equipment.

When all was completed, they crawled deep into their sleeping bags and fell asleep dreaming their dream - to cross Antarctica.

WACKY WEATHER

After reaching the top of the Sigyn Glacier, Ann and Liv began to climb the Antarctic Plateau, heading towards the South Pole. All was going according to plan and their spirits were high.

Suddenly, the wind they depended on to fill their sails and pull them into history disappeared. On Antarctica, normally the wind blows so hard it can blow people off their feet!

With the wind, they could travel 60 miles/96 kilometers or more in a day. Without the wind, they had to pull their heavy sleds and could only go about 10 miles per day. So, when the wind disappeared, Ann and Liv began to worry.

The wind had a mind of its own. It was hiding - where, they did not know, and it decided when and where it would blow. But, Ann and Liv did not give up. They skied and pulled and pulled with even more determination than ever to make their dream come true - to cross Antarctica!

TO THE RESCUE

After many days without wind, Ann and Liv were very worried, for they knew they must hurry. Then, they remembered they were not alone on their journey. They appealed to people around the world who were riding along with them.

"Help, we need wind! Please do a wind dance or sing a wind song - do something!" they pleaded.

Around the globe, children danced and Girl Scouts® sang! Parents wrote notes to the wind gods, men and women had private chats with Mother Nature and people prayed! The explorers even did wind dances. They danced like nobody was watching. And, good thing nobody was because Ann and Liv are much better polar explorers than dancers! And, low and behold, the wind began to blow.

Ann and Liv threw on their skis, put up their sails and off toward the South Pole they flew. They sailed, and sailed and pulled and sailed, focused on their dream - to cross Antarctica!

SOUTH POLE ARRIVAL - THE 64th DAY

On a gust of wind into the South Pole they blew. They were moving so fast, they nearly sailed right past the Pole. "Whoa, Nelly," they thought!

Their arrival came not a moment too soon, for their food was running low and they were falling behind schedule. At the Pole, more food and supplies were waiting for them.

Hastily, Ann and Liv packed their sleds and took a hot shower for the first time in more than 60 days. Then, as quickly as they had sailed into the South Pole, they sailed out in pursuit of their dream - to cross Antarctica!

NORTH TO McMURDO

Ann and Liv sailed away from the South Pole and headed North across the Titan Dome toward the Shackleton Glacier. The going was not easy. Not only did the wind continue to be uncooperative, the explorers also had to deal with raging blizzards and whiteouts that made it difficult for them to tell where the sky ended and the ground began.

Climbing down the Shackleton Glacier proved to be very treacherous. Liv tore a hole in her sled dragging it across a very sharp section of ice. They stopped to repair the sled and decided it was safer to take a detour away from the sharp ice and into an area where the ice was smoother.

Soon they were back on track and headed toward their dream - to cross Antarctica.

ACHIEVING HISTORY - DAY **90**

On February 12, 2001, the 90th day of their journey, Ann and Liv made history by reaching the Ross Ice Shelf, the place where the Antarctic land mass ends and the frozen sea begins. They became the first women ever to ski across Antarctica. When the world heard the news, they stood and cheered, some even teared.

For Ann and Liv it was a moment of mixed emotions. While overjoyed by their achievement, part of their dream was to ski across the frozen sea to McMurdo, a scientific research station on the coast of Antarctica. They knew part of their dream was fading fast with the summer sunlight on Antarctica.

However, they continued to ski and pull and sail and ski toward their dream - to cross Antarctica!

TOUGH DECISIONS - DAY 93

Finally, 93 days into their journey, Ann and Liv realized they could not reach McMurdo in time to catch the ship that was going to take them home. 475 miles/760 kilometers of ice stretched out between them and their final destination. Not even the wind dances or wind songs could help them now.

The Antarctic winter was beginning to set in and the ocean could freeze, trapping the ship and the explorers on Antarctica for the long, dark winter. The most difficult decision of the journey had to be made. So with heavy hearts, Ann and Liv decided to call for a plane to come and pick them up. They knew that not only did they need to consider their own safety, but the safety of those who would take them home.

For the last time on Antarctica they took off their skis and put away their sails - their ultimate dream now a part of history.

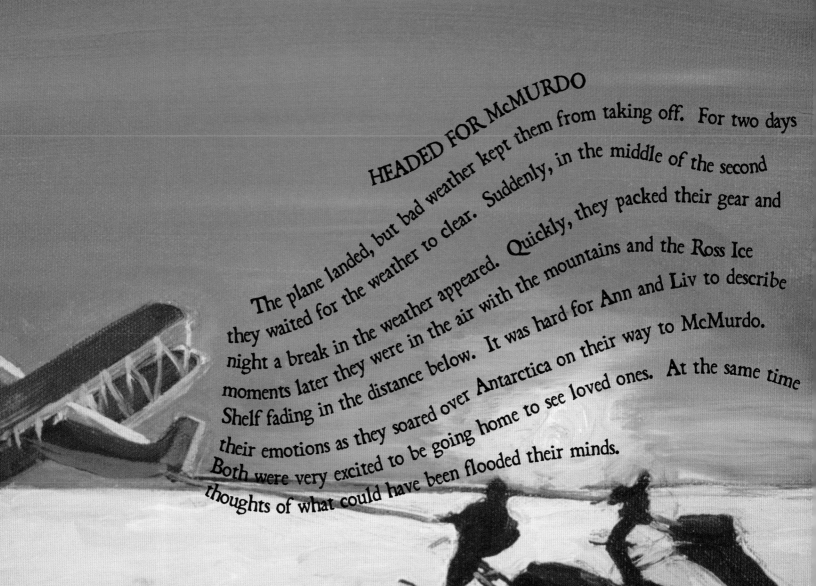

HEADED FOR McMURDO

The plane landed, but bad weather kept them from taking off. For two days they waited for the weather to clear. Suddenly, in the middle of the second night a break in the weather appeared. Quickly, they packed their gear and moments later they were in the air with the mountains and the Ross Ice Shelf fading in the distance below. It was hard for Ann and Liv to describe their emotions as they soared over Antarctica on their way to McMurdo. Both were very excited to be going home to see loved ones. At the same time thoughts of what could have been flooded their minds.

THE 97TH DAY - HOMEWARD BOUND

At McMurdo, Ann and Liv boarded a ship named Sir Hubert Wilkins that would take them to Australia, where they would board a plane bound for home.

On the ship, Ann and Liv took time to enjoy the sight of Emperor Penguins flapping their wings, and floating icebergs the size of skyscrapers.

PAYING HOMAGE

They made one more stop before leaving Antarctica. They took a moment to visit the huts left by two of their heroes, fellow explorers Ernest Shackleton and Robert F. Scott. They felt honored to pay tribute to the men who had inspired them.

As they walked back to the ship, it occurred to Ann and Liv that after all the planning and the training, the skiing and the sailing, and the laughter and the tears, they had turned their dream into another magnificent part of Antarctica's incredible history.

Ann and Liv stepped back onto the boat, proud of their accomplishments, knowing they had inspired others.

And, they sailed for home dreaming of their next expedition!

VegetablesCheeseA chair

Fresh fruit - Family and friends -

The newspaper - Pets - A shower

FOOD FACTS

- Ann and Liv each consumed approximately 4,500 calories per day.
- 45% of the calories, or 2,025 calories, came from fat.
- Ann and Liv added extra vegetable oil to their oatmeal and freeze dried dinners in order to increase the fat content.
- Liv's favorite foods: Walnut ice cream, Jarlsberg cheese, salads, seafood and fruit.
- Ann's favorite foods: Potatoes, fresh asparagus from the woods, vegetables from her garden, chocolate and hot fudge sundaes.

ANN AND LIV'S PAST EXPEDITIONS

LIV

1992: Led the first unsupported women's expedition across the Greenland Ice Cap.

1994: First woman to ski solo to the South Pole.

1996: Climbed Mt. Everest to 22,960 feet/7,000 meters.

ANN

1986: First woman to the North Pole.

1992: Climbed Mt. McKinley in Alaska.

1993: Led American Women's Expedition to the South Pole.

ANN AND LIV

2001: First women to ski across the continent of Antarctica.

DRAW YOUR DREAM!

THE GOLD RUSH
A PRIMARY SOURCE HISTORY OF THE SEARCH FOR GOLD IN CALIFORNIA

KERRI O'DONNELL

rosen central
Primary Source

To Ken and Catherine for instilling in me a love of words and history,
to Erin for encouraging me to share it,
and to Jeff Rucker for making me laugh all the while

Published in 2003 by The Rosen Publishing Group, Inc.
29 East 21st Street, New York, NY 10010

First Edition

Library of Congress Cataloging-in-Publication Data

O'Donnell, Kerri, 1972–
The gold rush : a primary source history of the search for gold in California / Kerri O'Donnell.—1st ed.
p. cm. — (Primary sources in American history)
Summary: Uses primary source documents, narrative, and illustrations to recount how the mid-nineteenth century California gold rush affected Americans and immigrants and how it shaped history.
Includes bibliographical references and index.
ISBN 0-8239-3682-1 (lib. bdg.)
1. California—Gold discoveries—Sources—Juvenile literature. 2. California—History—1846-1850—Sources—Juvenile literature. 3. Frontier and pioneer life—California—Sources—Juvenile literature. 4. Pioneers—California—History—19th century—Sources—Juvenile literature. [1. California—Gold discoveries—Sources. 2. California—History—1846-1859—Sources. 3. Frontier and pioneer life—California—Sources. 4. Pioneers—California.] I. Title. II. Series.
F865 .O36 2002
979.4'03—dc21
2002001367

Manufactured in the United States of America

CONTENTS

INTRODUCTION

The story of California's gold rush has all the aspects of a great drama. Countless characters crossed large distances to fulfill their dreams of obtaining riches in the golden land of "El Dorado." Although the gold rush technically began on January 24, 1848, when James Marshall discovered gold in a California river, it's necessary to examine California's political, cultural, and economic history to understand the consequences this event had on the development of California and the United States.

EL DORADO

By 1769, Spain had established its presence in the southernmost region of Mexico's California territory, near what is now San Diego. Spain wanted to protect its colonies in Mexico from invasion by other European empires that were anxious to acquire North American land. The California region had a lot to offer to the Spanish: The land could support different kinds of crops, and the Native American peoples living there could be colonized under Spanish rule. The colony of California grew very slowly in the decades that followed. Because California was so far away from the seat of power of Spain's colonial empire, it was difficult to keep it well-supplied. As a result, California attracted few new settlers.

Spain's colonial government was overthrown in 1821, and the republic of Mexico was established. Mexico opened California's ports to American and British merchants, and California became an important component of international trade. England, France, Russia, and the United States became fixated on California's natural resources. By the 1840s, emigrants from the East Coast of the United States began to travel to California, blazing transcontinental trails along the way. By 1845, many of these pioneers had settled in California's interior regions. These settlers found themselves under Mexican rule, but they did not want to give up their United States citizenship. Many settlers lobbied for the United States to annex California, rallying behind the idea that it was the United States's destiny to expand to the natural geographic limits of North America, from East Coast to West Coast.

Tensions grew between Mexico and the United States, further stoked by news of fighting between Mexican and American troops in Texas. Texas became a state in 1845, after years of fighting Mexico for it. War over the California territory (the last great expanse of land still technically owned by Mexico) seemed inevitable. The Mexican-American War was declared by the U.S. Congress on May 13, 1846, and lasted for nearly two years, but the United States's occupation of California during this time was for the most part uncontested. The war officially ended on February 2, 1848, with the United States victorious. California was now a U.S. territory.

James Marshall had found gold just days before the war ended, and news of the discovery began to spread. Soon everyone was clamoring for California's riches. The great rush to California's goldfields from points around the globe would change the face of California and transform the United States, a young country still grappling with the growing pains of its fairly new independence.

TIMELINE

1839 — John Sutter arrives in California and convinces governor Juan Bautista Alvarado to give him a land grant for 48,000 acres.

July 1845 — James Wilson Marshall arrives at Sutter's Fort after traveling on a wagon train from Oregon.

May 13, 1846 — U.S. Congress declares war on Mexico.

July 1846 — Although the Mexican-American War still rages, the United States flag is raised on Yerba Buena Island in San Francisco Bay.

August 1847 — John Sutter hires James Marshall to build a sawmill in Coloma, California.

January 24, 1848 — Marshall finds gold in a stream near Sutter's Mill.

February 2, 1848 — The Mexican-American War ends with the signing of the Treaty of Guadalupe Hidalgo. California is now an official U.S. territory.

March 15, 1848 — Marshall's discovery of gold appears in a San Francisco newspaper. It is largely ignored.

May 1848 — First wave of gold miners arrive at Sutter's Fort.

TIMELINE

June 1848 — Colonel Richard B. Mason, military governor of California, tours Coloma and confirms that there is gold there.

December 5, 1848 — President James K. Polk delivers the news of California's gold to Congress.

February 1849 — First shipload of miners arrives in San Francisco Bay aboard the vessel *California*.

May 1849 — First overland wagon trains begin their transcontinental journey west to California.

1850 — Territory of California officially becomes the thirty-first state.

March 14, 1851 — Foreign miners' tax is repealed.

June 9, 1851 — San Francisco Committee of Vigilance is formed.

September 1851 — San Francisco Committee of Vigilance is dissolved.

1852 — Gold becomes hard to find. Many miners return to their homes. Women and children arrive in large numbers to join their husbands and fathers in California.

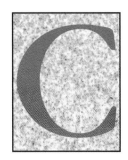

CHAPTER 1

THE GREAT DISCOVERY

In January 1848, a handyman named James Wilson Marshall made a discovery in a California river that would change the course of American history. On that winter morning, Marshall was going about his business, working for his employer, Johann Augustus Sutter. Sutter had assigned Marshall the task of overseeing construction of a sawmill. What Marshall found in the river near the mill would change both men's lives—and indeed the entire country—forever. Marshall had found gold.

The pencil sketch shown on page 9 was done by Marshall's own hand, and it illustrates what is widely considered the most important event in California's history—Marshall's discovery of gold at Sutter's Mill. Although the exact date of the sketch is unknown, it is clear that Marshall drew it soon after finding the gold. On the lower right-hand side of the sketch, Marshall wrote, "Situation of all hands on the mill at the

This sketch was found in James Marshall's cabin near Placerville, California. A man named John Sipp bought the property after Marshall's death in 1885. Sipp found the sketch in Marshall's desk, along with a map showing the site where Marshall had discovered the gold, part of the surrounding valley, and the sawmill itself. Sipp gave both the sketch and the map to the California State Library in 1910.

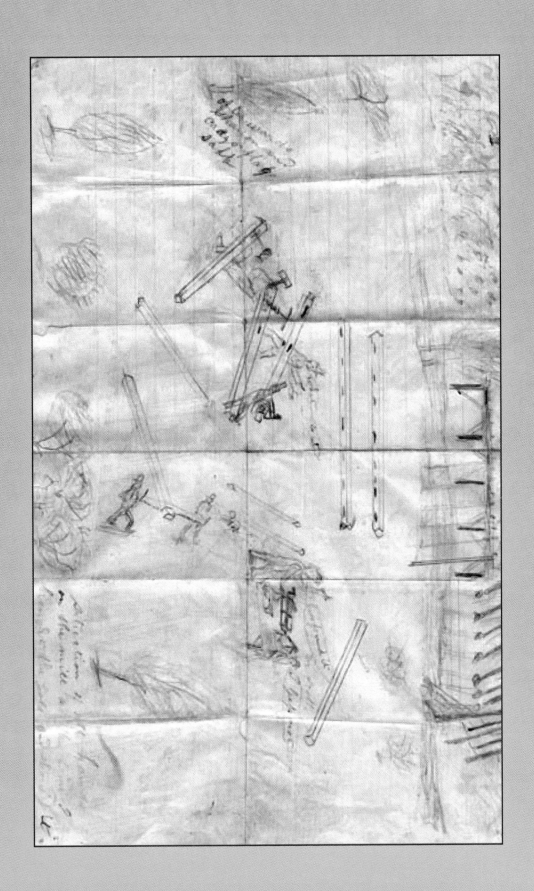

9

time I brought the gold and show'd it." A mill worker on the left-hand side of the drawing notes, "What is it?" Marshall, at the right, responds, "I have found it." A carpenter named William Scott, to the right of Marshall, says, "I guess not." According to historians, it is likely that the sketch re-creates the dialogue that took place at the mill immediately following Marshall's discovery.

The gold in that California river might have gone undiscovered if Marshall had not come to work for Johann Sutter—or John Sutter, as he came to be known. Sutter was a Swiss businessman who had come to America to make his fortune. After pursuing many unsuccessful business ventures, Sutter settled in California in 1839. At that time, California was part of the Mexican territory. Sutter persuaded California's governor, Juan Bautista Alvarado, to give him a land grant of nearly 50,000 acres in California's northern Central Valley. Here, on a piece of the land where the Sacramento and American Rivers meet, he built what came to be known as Sutter's Fort.

Sutter's Fort became the headquarters for his business ventures. He tried his hand at farming and raising livestock, hoping to strike it rich by supplying the public with flour, beef, and leather. Sutter needed people to work for him, so he employed groups of Native American laborers—such as the Yalisumni Nisenan Indians—who were from the area. Sutter paid them with items they needed, such as blankets, clothing, and tools. When he couldn't find enough manpower, he sometimes rounded up the Indians by force and made them work at gunpoint. Sutter also needed workers with the skills necessary to make his new "colony" self-sufficient. He needed men who could build new workshops so he could increase production and expand his empire. His plan was to build a town near Sutter's Fort, a place where settlers from the East could build their homes and thus spend their money on his merchandise. At Sutter's, one could buy saddles, blankets, hats, and shoes, among other items. The problem of finding enough workers was solved as more people began to migrate west during the 1840s.

James Marshall, one such immigrant, was an experienced craftsman who could carry out complex jobs. A new town would need lumber, and Sutter wanted to establish himself as the leading lumber supplier in the region. Marshall began working for Sutter, overseeing the building of a sawmill to process lumber. In August 1847, Marshall found the ideal spot for Sutter's Mill—the small town of Coloma. Coloma was on the southern part of the American River, about forty miles east of Sutter's Fort.

The sawmill was finished in January 1848. Marshall's men had begun deepening the stream near the mill to allow more water to flow to the mill wheel, which would increase the waterpower the mill needed to operate. On the morning of January 24, 1848, Marshall went down to the river to see how work was progressing. As he stood there, he saw a shining flash of light in the ditch, and he reached down to see what it was. It was gold.

Because Marshall was such an important part of California's history, many books were written about his life. One book, *The Life and Adventures of James W. Marshall, The Discoverer of Gold in California*, was written by George Frederick Parsons, and it is considered one of the most important historical books about California. On page 12, the title page from the book is shown. The illustration on the title page depicts Marshall holding a nugget of gold in his hand.

After Marshall made the discovery, he quickly went to tell Sutter the news. At first, Sutter didn't believe Marshall, but he

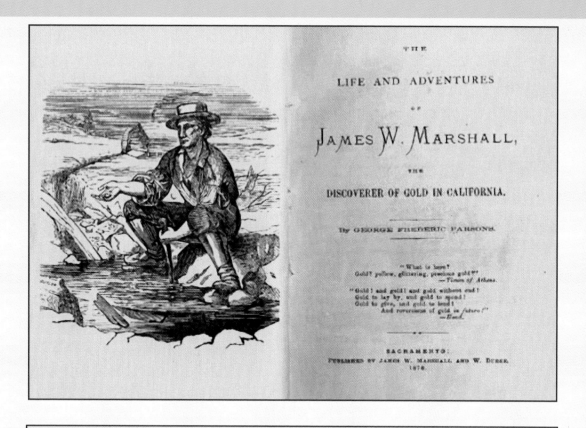

George Frederick Parsons wrote the 188-page book *The Life and Adventures of James W. Marshall, The Discoverer of Gold in California*, using information that was given to him by William Burke, one of James Marshall's business partners. Marshall and Burke had the book published in 1870 in Sacramento, California, as a way of drumming up public interest in Marshall's lecture tours. The book discusses Marshall's discovery of gold, but it also tells of his life of hard luck. Marshall often said that he believed he had been cursed and was doomed to suffer life's many disappointments. Marshall hoped that the book would win him favor with members of the state legislature and that they would grant him a pension. Despite his efforts, Marshall died a poor man in 1885.

EXCERPT FROM THE TITLE PAGE OF *THE LIFE AND ADVENTURES OF JAMES W. MARSHALL*

"What is here?
Gold? yellow, glittering, precious gold?"
　　　　　　　—Timon of Athens

"Gold! and gold! and gold without end!
Gold to lay by, and gold to spend!
Gold to give, and gold to lend!
And reversions of gold in future!"

quickly changed his mind when Marshall threw a handful of golden flakes on a nearby table. Marshall led Sutter to the sawmill, and Sutter inspected the site himself, using his knife to extract a lump of gold from a nearby gorge.

John Sutter's account of his fateful meeting with Marshall, and of their trip to the site the following day, was first seen in the *San Francisco Pacific News* on October 9, 1849, shown on page 14. At the top center is a portrait of James Marshall. Beneath that is a drawing of Sutter's Mill. Although Marshall and Sutter intended to keep the discovery secret, this proved impossible. Sutter writes: "Notwithstanding our precautions not to be observed, as soon as we came back to the mill, we noticed the excitement of the working people . . . and to complete our disappointment, one of the Indians who had worked at the gold mine . . . cried out in showing to us some specimens which he picked up by himself— Oro!-Oro-Oro!!!"

The Indians had also found *oro*—gold—and the news would soon spread throughout the land.

A few weeks before Marshall found the gold, Sutter and Marshall had tried to establish control of Coloma and the surrounding valley for their business plans. On January 1, 1848, just twenty-three days before Marshall found gold on the land, a lease was drafted so Sutter and Marshall could proceed without interruption. With Marshall's discovery of gold, control of the land became even more important. Sutter knew he had to control the Coloma Valley to keep his hands on the gold. He also knew that if a swarm of hopeful gold miners arrived, construction of his sawmill and a proposed gristmill would be delayed. He asked the construction crew to keep Marshall's discovery quiet, promising that they would be given time off to search for their own gold.

John Sutter's account of the events following Marshall's gold discovery was made into a letter sheet—stationery that could be personalized with a message and then folded and sealed to form its own envelope for mailing. This lithographed letter sheet was published in 1854 by San Francisco–based publishers Britton & Rey. The publishing company wanted to profit from Marshall's and Sutter's fame, and hoped that people who had come west would use the stationery to write to their loved ones in the East.

14

Along with John Sutter's and James Marshall's signatures, this lease bears the signatures of two chiefs and two *alcaldes* from the Yalisumni Indians. An *alcalde* was a head administrative and judicial officer of a Spanish town. It is believed that the original lease was destroyed in a fire. This copy remains at the California State Library and is part of the George McKinstry Collection. During the 1840s, George McKinstry worked for Sutter at Sutter's Fort in California's northern Central Valley. For a transcription and contemporary English translation, see page 56.

Sutter and Marshall met with leaders of the Yalisumni Nisenan Indian tribe to negotiate a lease for use of their tribal land in the Coloma Valley. The lease (shown above) had originally been drafted on January 1, 1848, but was not signed until February 4, 1848—eleven days after Marshall had discovered the gold, and just two days after the United States had defeated Mexico in the Mexican-American War and taken control of California. Sutter wanted the approval of the military governor of California, Colonel Richard Barnes Mason. He sent Mason the lease, but Mason quickly rejected it, stating in a letter to Sutter, "The United States do not recognize the right of Indians to sell or lease lands on which they reside."

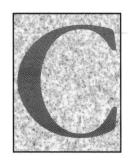

CHAPTER 2

During the winter and spring of 1848, news of Marshall's discovery spread throughout California. Men working for Sutter abandoned their jobs to search for gold, digging along the American River and its tributaries. In May 1848, news of gold reached San Francisco, along with a sample of gold dust that was promptly displayed in public. This touched off "gold fever," and large numbers of prospectors began to arrive in the area. These gold-seeking prospectors were called argonauts, a reference to Greek mythology. In Greek mythology, a man named Jason went on a quest for the Golden Fleece, a fleece made of gold that a king had placed in a grove guarded by a fierce dragon. Jason's crew, the Argonauts (named for the ship they sailed in, the *Argo*), assisted him in his voyage. In 1848, a quest had begun—not for the Golden Fleece of Greek mythology, but for the gold of California. As the San Francisco paper the *Californian* noted in its May 29, 1848, edition, "The whole country, from San Francisco to Los Angeles, and from the sea shore to the base of the Sierra Nevadas, resounds with the sordid cry, 'gold, GOLD, GOLD!' while the field is left half planted, the house half built, and everything neglected but the manufacture of shovels and pickaxes."

News of the gold soon spread throughout the United States, across the Atlantic Ocean to Europe via ships, south into Mexico

GOLD FEVER

and South America, and west across the Pacific Ocean via trading vessels bound for Hawaii, China, and Australia. Marshall's discovery would lead to a massive migration. At first, most of the gold seekers who arrived in California were not from the United States. In 1848, there were no transcontinental telegraph lines or railroads that would allow for news to spread quickly across the country, and the trip on foot was slow and painful. Most news spread via ocean-going vessels, but this was also a slow process.

The news of the gold in California traveled by ship south along the Pacific coast to the tip of South America, around Cape Horn, and then up the Atlantic Coast to the eastern port cities of the United States. This trip could take up to seven months. Another possible route for spreading the news was traveling down the Pacific coast by ship as far as the Isthmus of Panama— a thin piece of land that separates the Pacific Ocean from the Caribbean Sea. Passengers then went on foot across the isthmus, and another boat would take them through the Caribbean to the East Coast. Though shorter than the Cape Horn route, this approach also took many weeks.

A ship traveling to China or South America could complete a trip in less time. For this reason, people from other countries began to arrive in large numbers before people from the eastern United States even knew of the gold strike. When people in the eastern United States finally did hear the news, they often didn't believe the stories. In June 1848, California's military governor, Richard Barnes Mason, set out to examine the gold district to see if the stories coming out of Coloma Valley were true. He toured the land around the American River and prepared a report on the great quantities of gold found in the region and sent it to Washington, D.C., along with a chest filled with gold.

On December 5, 1848, in his inaugural address, President James Polk acknowledged the validity of the gold strike to Congress, and within days, the people of the eastern United States were overwhelmed by gold fever. For many, the only cure was to head west to seek their fortune. Many who made the journey later returned east to give lectures on the topic, which stirred up even more interest in California. The mass migration was under way.

Different publications further helped spread the stories of California's golden treasure. Some of these publications took the form of broadsheets—large sheets of paper printed on one or both sides that could be reproduced in large quantities. These were handed out to the public or posted in public places, usually to generate interest in a lecture or presentation by someone who had been to California's gold mines. People might be charged a small sum to attend, and both the lecturer and the event's organizer could make a nice profit.

Books about California's gold were quickly written. One such book was written by a man named J. Ely Sherwood, who had traveled to California and decided to share his experiences with the gold-hungry public. His book, shown on page 19—written in 1849 and published in New York—was entitled *The Pocket Guide to California; A Sea and Land Route Book, Containing a Description of the El Dorado . . . To Which Is Added the Gold-Hunter's Memorandum and Pocket Directory.* The book's long title mirrors

Many books published during the gold rush used sensationalism to sell copies. J. Ely Sherwood's book was no exception. Along with the hard facts about California, Sherwood included advertisements for all kinds of strange merchandise for the hopeful gold miner. He also mentioned a locomotive that would transport people from New York to California in three days, writing: "We advise our readers to look-out for the fast line." The first transcontinental railroad, however, did not operate until May 1869.

THE

POCKET GUIDE TO CALIFORNIA;

A

SEA AND LAND ROUTE BOOK,

CONTAINING

A DESCRIPTION OF THE EL DORADO; ITS GEOGRAPHICAL POSITION;
PEOPLE, CLIMATE, SOIL, PRODUCTIONS, AGRICULTURAL
RESOURCES, COMMERCIAL ADVANTAGES,
AND MINERAL WEALTH;

WITH

A CHAPTER ON GOLD FORMATIONS;

ALSO THE

CONGRESSIONAL MAP,

AND

THE VARIOUS ROUTES AND DISTANCES TO THE GOLD REGIONS.

TO WHICH IS ADDED THE

Gold-Hunter's Memorandum and Pocket Directory.

BY J. E. SHERWOOD.

" Westward the course of Empire takes its way."—Berkeley.

⸻ • • ⸻

NEW YORK:

J. E. SHERWOOD, PUBLISHER AND PROPRIETOR.

FOR SALE BY H. LONG & BROTHER, 46 ANN STREET; BERFORD & CO.,
ASTOR HOUSE; AND THE PRINCIPAL BOOKSELLERS THROUGHOUT
THE UNION.

CALIFORNIA: BERFORD & CO., AND C. W. HOLDEN, SAN FRANCISCO.

1849.

the extensive information contained within the book—a discussion of the various routes to California by land and by sea, a description of California's geographical features, and a summation of California's "people, climate, soil, productions, agricultural resources, commercial advantages, and mineral wealth."

Only a few months had passed since James Marshall discovered gold, but hopeful gold seekers had all manner of written material on the subject at their fingertips. Books were published within months. Newspapers around the country jumped at the chance to use gold fever to sell papers in the winter of 1848–1849. The newspapers published story after story about the adventures of life out West, using every detail they could to fill their papers and meet their deadlines.

There were countless firsthand accounts of ship passengers and captains who had made the trek west, detailing the journey and the strange new land that met them upon arrival. There were stories from the goldfields by those already hard at work digging for riches, and there were also incredible tales of wealth beyond a person's wildest dreams. The newspapers published every official text available on the subject in order to convince people that the sometimes outrageous stories they were printing on their pages were true. All these things fueled the fire already burning in would-be argonauts' bellies and hastened their preparations for the journey west. Newspapers were also full of endless editorial commentary poking fun at the new national obsession with California's gold. On January 1, 1849, the lengthy poem on page 21 appeared in an eastern newspaper called the *Eastern Argus*. It takes a satirical look at the gold fever that gripped the eastern United States during this time.

CARRIERS' ADDRESS
TO THE PATRONS OF
THE EASTERN ARGUS.

JANUARY 1, 1849.

Come on good friends—all other things give o'er,
We'll talk of Gold, on California's shore.
Gold! the great end and aim of human strife;
The all-exciting stimulus of life.

O, Power Supreme! man's earliest offerings shine
As votive gifts around thy glittering shrine.
Forever kneeling at thy altars proud,
Behold a suppliant, fawning, cringing crowd,
There offering up peace, honor, virtue, health,
To gain an entrance to the heaven of wealth.
Time was—time is—when gold's almighty sway
The high and low—the small and great obey.
It changes ill to good, and wrong to right;
Makes the *disgusting* fill us with delight.
The mean and grovelling are, presto! made
Noble and generous, by its potent aid.
Tinged with its glare, the basest crimes assume
To mortal eyes the hue of virtue's bloom;
Changes the prate of fools to sayings good!—
Makes dulness wit, *not always understood!*
Base deeds it makes a mark of souls refined,
And "asses' ears," signs of a noble mind.
The vain and ignorant it makes the great,—
To fools' opinions adds its mighty weight;
While Solomon himself without a "shiner"
Would only be a foolish "penny a liner."
A *beast* that has it, with the gods is ranged,
A man without it to a beast is changed.
So by the almighty influence of gold
Fashion and morals both are thus controlled.
A line is drawn between the rich and poor,
Which no presumptuous mortal must pass o'er.
Give me but gold, you give me virtue, wisdom, grace,
Raise me at once to fashion's highest place;
And saints and sinners bow down and adore—
Not me in truth, but my rich glittering ore.
No wonder then the world is going mad—
No wonder then that thousand hearts are glad
To hear of regions in the far-off West,
With all untold, unthought-of treasures blest;
Where mother earth her golden treasures yields
Not to such toil as tills New England fields,
But places free before her outstretched hand
Her stores exhaustless of the glittering sand.

Go then, ye slaves, to California's shore
Go delve and dig, and grasp the precious ore.
Leave home and friends, and all the heart holds dear,
There seek a comfort for each sorrow here,
Find all it needs, to make you rich and great,
To live in more than Dives' royal state,
To every want and every wish supply,
And then, poor delvers, give it up—and die!
While greedy heirs, expectant for your death,
With greedy eyes, shall watch your passing breath,
With outward woe, but inward joy profound,
Behold you safely nestled in the ground.
Well, you may die—your heirs possess your gains—

But still exhaustless from those distant plains,
With ceaseless flow, on rolls a golden tide
Till the most craving wishes are supplied;
Till, Midas-like, gold only meets our sight,
And sun and moon shine with a golden light.
Oh, what a change—all will be rich and great,
Will live at ease in more than royal state.
Ogle's *spoon* vision then will prove to be
A bright glance forward to futurity.
He thought he saw *gold* spoons—'t was but a glance
Of coming days, of one in prophet's trance.
Man's hateful bondage now forever o'er,
He'll think to work and toil, and slave no more.
No more aristocrats there'll be, for all
Will then alike be most "amazing tall."
No dandies then—for tailors sure will cease
Their skilful labors to make others please,
But strange to tell, each his own work must do:
No gold could hire a man to make a shoe.
Gold plate and spoons will then too vulgar be,
In fashion's realms such things you'll no more see;
The "exclusive's" style will be plain *iron* ware,
And iron rings to adorn their fingers fair.
The suffering exquisite will then be vain
To sport his iron stud and iron chain;
Rich folks, with us so common then you'll see,
The poor—the Lions of the day will be.

* * * * * *

Since gold engrosses now our every thought,
" Niggers and Rum" and politics' forgot,
We've talked of gold—but ere we close our rhymes
We'll say a word or two about the times.
This year another President will see,
But whether "Old Whitey" or "Old Zack" it be,
Not half of those who chose him care or know,
If either would the offices bestow.
Upon a hungry, greedy, clamorous crowd,
For either, they would shout their pæans loud.
But even now, a darkling cloud appears,
The distant thunder bursts upon our ears,
And gathering masses rising thick and fast,
Portend the fury of the storm at last.
For one poor office hundreds will contend,
And all but one be furious in the end;
And then on all-important measures too,
Alas! old Zack, what can your party do?
Believing that in politics all's fair,
They've promised one thing here—another there.
To some a tariff, and to some "free soil,"
And all to have at least some share of spoil.
Ah, yes! the storm is gathering sure and past,—
Let it come on! 't will soon be over fast—
DEMOCRACY's pure sun, all bright and glorious,
Shine forth o'er whigs and whiggery victorious.

* * * * * *

Just one word more to patrons new and old,
We wish *health, happiness,* and *mines of gold!*

The third stanza of "Carriers' Address" mentions "Dives," recalling the story of Dives and Lazarus from the Bible. Dives was a rich man who dressed in fancy clothes and enjoyed great feasts, while Lazarus, a poor man, lay starving in front of his house. After their deaths, Lazarus went to heaven, but Dives was sent to hell to be tortured for eternity. The parable teaches that those who seek nothing but riches on Earth will spend eternity paying for their greed, while the poor will be rewarded in heaven. See page 57 for a partial transcription of the poem.

21

Come on good friends—all other things give o'er,
We'll talk of Gold, on California's shore,
Gold! The great end and aim of human strife;
The all-exciting stimulus of life . . .
Go then, ye slaves, to California's shore
Go delve and dig, and grasp the precious ore.

The writer expressed the opinion that the nation's obsession with riches had made people forget the truly important things in life. People were now "slaves" to gold and had given up everything that was truly good in life to find it.

Satirical views of the gold rush found their way into every aspect of American life. Artists used humorous drawings to convey their opinions about how the obsession with California's gold was affecting the politics, economy, and spirit of the United States. Many saw gold fever as a disease infecting the morality of the entire nation, a growing greed that was making people neglect their ideals and values in order to make a quick fortune.

In the 1849 lithograph by Nathaniel Currier shown on the facing page, a subtitle reads: "An accurate drawing of the famous hill of gold, which has been put into a scow by the owner, and attached to a Sperm Whale who is now engaged in towing it around the Horn for New York." The man in the cartoon sits high atop a mound of gold that has been placed in a scow, a kind of flat-bottomed boat used mainly to haul large quantities of raw materials or garbage. The man—shown in typical upper-class attire, complete with top hat and umbrella—represents a stereotypical greedy "Yankee" from New York, intent on lugging home the vast riches he has accumulated in "El Dorado," the golden land of California.

This lithograph, entitled *California Gold*, is attributed to Nathaniel Currier (1813–1888). Currier was a partner in a famous New York City art firm called Currier and Ives. The firm specialized in publishing lithographs and enjoyed great fame in the mid to late 1800s. It produced more than 7,000 works during this time. The lithographs served as an artistic view of life in America during this period, touching on a vast array of subjects: historical events, politics, fashion, sports, disasters, and even celebrities. At that time, the lithographs were very affordable. Today, many of the more rare lithographs have become valuable collectors' items.

DIALOGUE IN THE CARTOON:

I'll be darned to darnation if this haint the greatest Blower I ever did drive in harness anyhow—I rather think he goes his mile a leetle inside one minit; what a darned fool I was not to take some passengers—they'd have paid the expenses praps and maybee a leetle more.—

CONTEMPORARY ENGLISH:

I'll be darned if this isn't the best whale I've ever driven—I think he goes a mile in less than a minute. I was a fool not to take some passengers on board—perhaps they would have covered the cost of the trip and maybe even given me a little more.

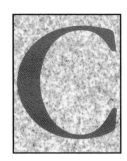

CHAPTER 3

TO CALIFORNIA BY SEA

Once gold fever hit the East, there was no stopping it. People headed to California in huge numbers. After President Polk's address to Congress in late 1848, an estimated 1,400 vessels soon set sail for California from the United States and Canada alone. Easterners from the seafaring cities and towns of New England and the Mid-Atlantic states usually made the journey by ship, heading out from the nearest port. They were often called "forty-niners," a reference to the year 1849, when they left their lives behind in search of gold.

As more Easterners headed west, the results of the mass migration to California were felt strongly in smaller eastern communities where the population was noticeably reduced. The island of Nantucket, off the coast of Massachusetts, was one such community. During the late 1700s, Nantucket had become one of the world's largest

A twenty-four page book was published on January 1, 1850, by a man named Jethro C. Brock of Nantucket, Massachusetts. It provides a listing of 650 people from Nantucket Island, Massachusetts, who had gone to California or were en route there at the beginning of 1850. The book provides a list of the ship names that had left for California, as well as their departure and arrival schedules. The last page of the book gives a listing of people who had come back to Nantucket, as well as eight people who died either while in California or on their way there. Shown here is the cover.

A LIST

OF

Persons from Nantucket

NOW IN

CALIFORNIA,

OR ON THEIR WAY THITHER;

INCLUDING

THE NAMES OF THE VESSELS IN WHICH THEY SAILED, THE TIME OF SAILING, AND OF THEIR ARRIVAL THERE;

ALSO,

PERSONS RETURNED, &c,

NANTUCKET:

PUBLISHED BY JETHRO C. BROCK.

January 1, 1850.

whaling centers. By 1850, many people from the area had set out to find gold.

Some Easterners sailed south, down the eastern coast, around Cape Horn at the southernmost tip of South America, and then up the Pacific coast, finally reaching San Francisco Bay—a trip that could be as long as 18,000 nautical miles from start to finish. It is estimated that as many as 16,000 people traveled to California via the Cape Horn route in 1849, followed by about 12,000 more people in 1850. Those who wanted a quicker voyage chose a route that combined both sea and land travel. They sailed to the Isthmus of Panama, where they would cross the narrow strip of land on foot and board a northbound ship for the trip up the Pacific coast to California.

On page 27 is a typical map of the period. It shows the main water routes that were traveled to reach California from the East—either around Cape Horn or through the Isthmus of Panama, also known as Chagres. The western part of the United States is shown on the left, and Central and South America appear on the right. The yellow-shaded area shows the region where gold was found. Included on the map are two text boxes. The text box on the left is entitled "Important Directions to Persons Emigrating to California." The box on the right is entitled "Description of California, or the New Gold Region," and contains the following words: "Such is California—the richest, most picturesque and beautiful region, for its extent, upon the face of the earth."

The trip around Cape Horn by boat took about six months and brought passengers through dangerous waters. Upon reaching the waters around the horn, a ship would lurch because of the turbulent currents, and huge waves would crash over the deck. The winds were freezing, and sometimes ships were blown farther

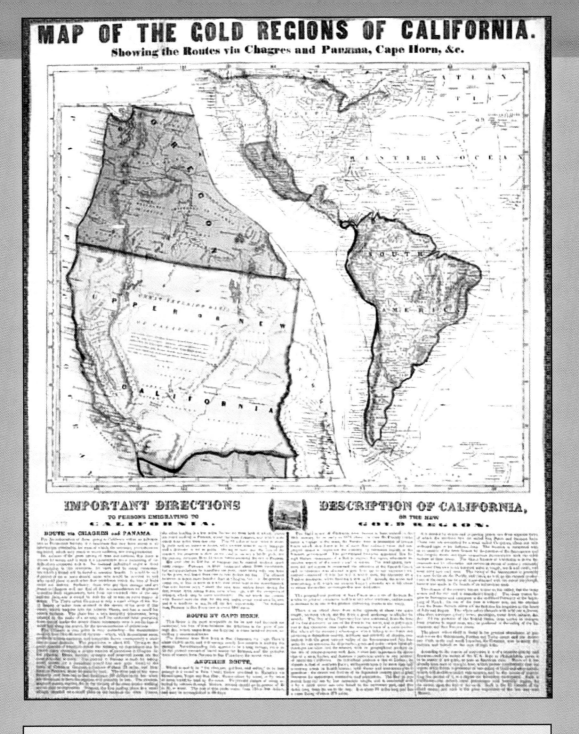

This map of the water routes to California was published in 1849 by Ensign & Thayer. It is a hand-colored lithograph measuring approximately sixteen inches by fourteen inches. It is now housed at the California State Library. This copy was originally inserted in a 1849 travel book by T. J. Farnham about his travels in California. The map was probably printed in larger quantities after the book was published and was included with the book to boost sales. People were hungry for any information about the journey west for gold, and the map would allow readers to see how they might make such a journey themselves.

south toward Antarctica. It usually took about a month to complete this part of the trip around the horn. The voyage was usually made by young men who were seeking adventure.

The route via the Isthmus of Panama was shorter and could be made in two months if there were no major delays, but it was also a difficult trip. Once ships from the East reached Panama, passengers had to travel about seventy-five miles up the Chagres River to cross the isthmus, then travel another twenty-five miles by mule through the jungle to get to Panama City. At Panama City, another ship would take them up the Pacific coast to California. During the first few years of the gold rush, there was a shortage of ships from Panama to San Francisco. This meant that thousands of people were left waiting for a ship to take them north to California. Some came down with yellow fever or malaria, diseases transmitted by mosquitoes, and many travelers contracted cholera and died while waiting for ships to San Francisco.

The seemingly endless days aboard ships bound for California were filled with other dangers, too. Many passengers got scurvy, a disease caused by a lack of vitamin C. It was difficult to keep up a supply of vitamin C–rich fruits and vegetables on the ship—these foods quickly went bad. Scurvy causes bleeding gums, loose teeth, and swollen, blackened legs. Chills and delirium often set in, and death sometimes followed.

Whether coming up along the Pacific coast from Cape Horn or from Panama, many ships had to sail out to the Sandwich Islands (now called Hawaii) before they could even catch the winds they needed to take them to the port of San Francisco. Boredom became an issue—after spending so much time at sea, passengers desperately needed some kind of entertainment. They became quite creative in finding ways to amuse themselves, putting out ship newspapers or staging plays to pass the time. Although the promise of gold was all most people needed to embark on a voyage west, some ship owners made up persuasive advertisements that listed all the comforts of their ships, hoping to fill their cabins with customers who would pay a lot for safe passage to California.

The broadsheet shown on page 30 was typical of the printed advertisements for ships sailing around Cape Horn to California. The trip to California aboard *Balance* cost each passenger $150, a hefty sum of money at the time. Included in that price were sleeping accommodations, meals, and "5 cubic feet [a three-dimensional measurement of a foot] of baggage or freight, without regard to its weight." The ship's owners, Brooks and Frye, also made sure to mention the following fact: "There will be no second cabin or steerage passengers to annoy the cabin passengers with their filth and disorder." ("Steerage" referred to a section of a ship with inferior accommodations that were occupied by passengers who paid the lowest fare.) This statement was likely made to attract an upper-class group of passengers who could pay a higher price for their passage. It was likely that they were glad to pay the high rate for a guarantee that they wouldn't have to share tight living quarters with lower-class passengers who had purchased steerage tickets.

As demand for transportation to the goldfields increased, so did the price. Soon, a ticket could cost between $500 and $1,000. To gold seekers, this seemed a small price to pay compared to the riches that they hoped lay waiting in California. In the months between April 1849 and January 1850, as many as 40,000 people may have reached San Francisco by sea to search for their fortunes. However, not everyone was in search of gold and material wealth. A few passengers among the throngs of gold seekers had

FOR CALIFORNIA, SAN FRANCISCO, AND THE GOLD MINES.

 SHIP  BALANCE.

The superior coppered and copper fastened Ship BALANCE, Capt. E. Washburn Ruggles, will be dispatched for the Sacramento and the Gold Mines, on the 18th day of January, 1849. The Ship is built of Live Oak and Teak, and is as strong and safe a ship as sails out of this port. She is a remarkably good sea boat, is perfectly tight, well found in sails and rigging, and with boats sufficient to carry all the passengers, and in all respects perfectly fitted for a safe, expeditious, and comfortable voyage around Cape Horn.

In a long voyage, particular attention ought to be paid to the comfort of the passengers, and the owners of the Ship flatter themselves that in this respect she presents unequalled attractions. She is provided with state-rooms throughout. The number of passengers is limited, giving ample room to all. There will be no second cabin or steerage passengers to annoy the cabin passengers by their filth and disorder. The cabin is light, airy, and well ventilated, and furnished in a style unequalled by any other vessel. The table and the provision departments will be under the supervision of a competent steward and his assistants, who will attend to laying in stores of everything that can be taken to sea, in order that the table may present a constant variety.

The owners of this vessel intend to go in the ship, thus affording to their passengers the best assurance that their arrangements will be complied with. The fare is fixed at as low a rate as it is possible where the promises made are intended to be kept.

Fare $150, for which the passenger is found with everything requisite for the voyage, and is entitled to carry 5 cubic feet of baggage or freight, without regard to its weight. And a preference will be given to freight carried by the passengers over any other that may offer. Families taken at a reasonable deduction. Consignments taken on liberal terms.

Applications for Freight or Passage may be made to Messrs. COOK & SMITH, 110 Wall-street, or to

B. S. BROOKS,
FREDERICK FRYE,

BROOKS & FRYE,
No. 10 Wall-street, N. Y.

NEW YORK, Dec. 26th, 1848.

This advertisement, which was likely posted around New York City on December 26, 1848, alerted the public of the sail date of the ship *Balance*, bound from New York City to Sacramento, California. The trip was to begin on January 18, 1849, under the command of Captain E. Washburn Ruggles. In the advertisement, Frederick Frye and B. S. Brooks list all of the features found on their ship. The ship, made of oak and teak, is described as follows: "She is a remarkably good sea boat, is perfectly tight . . . and in all respects perfectly fitted for a safe, expeditious, and comfortable voyage around Cape Horn."

This daguerreotype of Reverend Joseph A. Benton was made by an unknown artist. Although the date is unknown, the image shows Benton as he likely appeared to those to whom he preached aboard the *Edward Everett*. The *Edward Everett* set sail on January 11, 1849, and arrived in San Francisco Bay on July 6, 1849, which means that Reverend Benton had about six months to preach to the ship's passengers. He is shown seated in formal dress, perhaps the same clothing he wore when preaching to his congregation aboard the *Edward Everett*. Daguerreotypes like this one utilized an early photographic technique in which the image was produced on a silver plate, or on a copper plate covered in silver.

more idealistic reasons for making the trip west. One such passenger was Reverend Joseph A. Benton (pictured above), a Protestant clergyman who went to California to preach the word of God to the people there. Reverend Benton set sail from Boston aboard the *Edward Everett*, accompanying members of the Boston and California Joint Stock Mining and Trading Company.

During the long voyage, Reverend Benton not only preached sermons to the passengers but also held discussions on religious topics. He kept a diary aboard the ship as well as after he

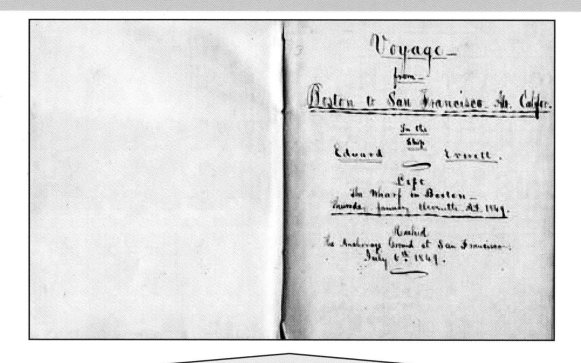

After Reverend Benton arrived in San Francisco Bay, he traveled inland. On July 14, 1849, he reached Sacramento, which he called "the city of tents and trees." That first day, according to Benton's diary, he set up camp under some oak trees. He established the First Church of Christ, also called the Pioneer Congregational Church. Benton delivered his first sermon there on July 22, 1849. About 100 men and three women gathered in the grove of trees to hear the sermon, which Benton delivered from his wagon. In his diary—so extensive that it takes up two volumes—Benton writes about his experiences with his congregation, which was largely made up of gold miners.

reached California. In it, he described his experience in detail. Pictured above is the title page from Benton's diary.

Upon the *Edward Everett*'s arrival in San Francisco, the sight that greeted Reverend Benton and the other passengers was likely much like the scene shown on page 33. In the months and years after Marshall discovered gold at Sutter's Mill, San Francisco became the prime destination of gold seekers from around the globe. Before Marshall's discovery, San Francisco had been a quiet

VIEW OF SAN FRANCISCO, CALIFORNIA.

This view of San Francisco, California, by William Birch McMurtrie (1816–1872) represents San Francisco Bay as seen from atop Telegraph Hill in April 1850. Nathaniel Currier, the New York City–based printer, published this hand-colored lithograph in 1851. McMurtrie was a well-known landscape, portrait, and survey artist of the period. Here, he depicts San Francisco's wharves and the abandoned ships anchored in Yerba Buena Cove—ships that had brought argonauts from far and wide to San Francisco Bay. Also shown are the prospectors' tents and rickety wooden shacks, and two ships, the *Apollo* and the *Niantic*, that had been converted into warehouses.

little port with a population of perhaps 1,000 people. Just a few years later, it had quickly grown into a boisterous city of nearly 30,000 people, most of them argonauts.

San Francisco didn't go through the many years of growth and development that most cities experienced. It became an instant city of canvas tents and hastily built wooden structures that provided only the most basic shelter for the anxious prospectors who arrived at San Francisco Bay.

CHAPTER 4

THE OVER- LANDERS

In the years preceding Marshall's discovery of gold, people from the East had been making their way west, mapping out routes across the continent toward Oregon and California. These pioneers crossed the grassy prairies of the plains, the treacherous passes of the Rocky Mountains, and the arid deserts, all the while transporting their possessions in wagons that often broke down or were lost in flooded rivers. It was a very difficult and often dangerous journey. Sickness and disease claimed many lives, and severe weather often took many more—or, at the very least, delayed travel and made living conditions miserable.

This letter sheet, *Hutchings' Panoramic Scenes—Crossing the Plains*, was published by James M. Hutchings in Placerville, California, around 1854. It features "views drawn from nature in 1853" by famous gold rush–era artist George Holbrook Baker, who lived from 1827 until 1906. In this famous work, Baker drew thirteen separate scenes depicting the experiences of overlanders crossing the plains on their way west along the Oregon Trail. The drawings give a good sense of what life was like for the overlanders. Baker depicts a wagon train against the backdrop of mountains, camps set up by weary overlanders, buffalo hunts that provided food, shelter, and clothing, and the livestock drives that kept farm animals moving along the trail. Baker also illustrates potentially dangerous meetings with Indians along the trail—usually members of the prairie tribes such as the Sioux and the Cheyenne—as well as prominent landmarks seen along the way, such as Scott's Bluff and Chimney Rock.

HUTCHINGS' PANORAMIC SCENES. — CROSSING THE PLAINS.

EMIGRANT TRAIN PASSING WIND RIVER MOUNTAINS

SIOUX INDIANS

COURT-HOUSE ROCK

CHIMNEY ROCK

LARAMIE PEAK

INDIANS CHASING BUFFALOES, SCOTT'S BLUFFS

FIRST NIGHT ON THE PLAINS

SCENE ON THE DESERT

STUCK FAST

MOUTH OF ASH HOLLOW

DEVIL'S GATE

CASTLE ROCK

Published by J. M. HUTCHINGS, Placerville. [Copyright secured.]   DRIVING STOCK ACROSS THE PLAINS   [Views drawn from Nature in 1855 by George H. Baker.

35

The overland routes that the pioneers had established became more crowded with migrating gold seekers. Many prospectors who didn't like the idea of a journey by sea took to the overland trails, earning the nickname "overlanders." The overlanders followed the lead of those who had made the journey by boat, often forming large joint-stock companies for the trip west. Technically, joint-stock companies were groups of people who got together to run a business, drawing from a joint stock of capital owned by individual members of the company. However, in the case of the overlanders, these companies banded together for a common purpose, sharing their resources in order to help one another reach California's goldfields.

Some joint-stock companies were arranged informally and often consisted of family members or groups of friends and neighbors. In large eastern cities like Boston, Philadelphia, and New York, companies sometimes formed when people responded to newspaper advertisements for overland treks to California. Once the companies were formed, the overlanders had to choose which transcontinental path they would take to ensure the quickest and least difficult journey. Many relied chiefly on the longest of the overland trails that the pioneers had blazed in the decade leading up to the gold rush—the Oregon Trail.

The Oregon Trail made its way through about 2,000 miles of plains, deserts, and mountains, beginning at Independence, Missouri, and ending in the Pacific Northwest. In the years following Marshall's discovery at Sutter's Mill, many groups of overlanders gathered near the Missouri River at Independence to start out on their journey west. Before the trip even began, many things had to be considered. Often, people had to camp on the Missouri River's eastern bank, waiting for spring vegetation to grow to avoid the risk of starving their animals. If they waited too long, however, they could be caught in the mountains when severe winter weather struck. This could mean freezing to death or starving if the animals died from the harsh elements or lack of food. Timing was crucial, and new difficulties would face them as they set out across the plains.

On a day without unexpected delays or difficulties, the wagon trains could cover about ten to fifteen miles. On a bad day, they might not even move an inch. Once on the trail, the travelers were on their own. Dangers had to be faced as a group, or all would fail. Any hardship—whether hunger, sickness, injury, severe weather, buffalo stampedes, or broken equipment—had to be overcome using whatever resources were available within the group, or with the help of a company that was close by on the trail. With only their fellow travelers to help them, the overlanders had to be prepared for anything.

The transcontinental travelers also made sure they were prepared to dig for gold and haul it away once they found it. They wanted to be sure they had every tool they would need in their quest for fortune. Many shopkeepers and merchants in towns along the westbound trails took advantage of the prospectors' enthusiasm, convincing them that they simply had to have certain items in order to strike it rich in California. While they did sell some necessary goods—oxen, mules, guns and gunpowder, and packsaddles—they also promoted worthless things such as "automatic gold washers" and "goldometers." Some merchants told the overlanders that they could trade these items with the Indians along the trail for gold.

The lithograph on page 39 pokes fun at the overlanders. The following dialogue appears on the top of some versions of the lithograph: "I am sorry I did not follow the advice of Granny and go around the Horn, through the Straights, or by Chagres," says the overlander. Rather than choosing the sea route and traveling around Cape Horn or via the Chagres River in Panama, this cartoon overlander represents all those unexperienced—or "greenhorn"—travelers who loaded themselves down with every imaginable appliance, items that usually had to be dumped along the trail later to lighten their loads. By autumn of 1849, it is possible that about 35,000 overlanders had made the journey to California, with perhaps 100,000 more people following them during the next few years. California was soon teeming with immigrants who set up camps and got to the business of mining for gold.

This lithograph by Henry R. Robinson was published (circa 1850) as a hand-tinted lithograph and in black and white by New York publishers Kellogg & Comstock and by Buffalo, New York, publishers Ensign & Thayer. Behind the gold hunter is a road sign pointing out that it is 350 miles to Saint Louis, where the overlander began his journey, and another 1,700 miles to California, where he is headed. This is a satirical look at the buying frenzy that took hold of many overlanders. The lithograph shows a man traveling to California, weighed down with many useless items. He is even shown wearing a large pan as a hat. His gentlemanly attire makes him look foolish; he's dressed much too grandly for the difficult journey ahead of him. The teapot hanging off the end of one of his tools shows just how overloaded the man is for the trip west. It is an item, like many of the items he carries, that he does not need.

THE INDEPENDENT GOLD HUNTER ON HIS WAY TO CALIFORNIA.
I NEITHER BORROW NOR LEND.

CHAPTER 5

LIFE IN THE MINES

Whether the argonauts got to California by land or sea, once they reached the golden land their lives were much the same—difficult. The first mining camps sprang up immediately after Marshall's discovery at Sutter's Mill. They consisted of clusters of canvas tents set up around the miners' claims. A claim was a tract of land that had been staked out by a miner as his own. The miners would rise with the sun, eat a sparse breakfast of biscuits and coffee, then spend the day digging for gold with a pick and shovel. Next, they would begin panning—putting dirt in a pan, adding water, and swishing the mixture around. Little by little, the dirt would wash over the pan's edge. If there was gold in the dirt, the gold would remain in the pan because it was heavier. It was a slow, painstaking process, and even if the miners found gold, they usually didn't find more than a few dollars' worth a day. As time passed, miners began to build new tools to help them sift through greater

This woodcut was produced by an unknown artist around 1854. On the left, a miner is using a cradle to separate gold from dirt. On the right, a man brings him buckets of water to add to the dirt. If a miner was near a river, it was easy to obtain the water needed to cradle. If a miner was in a dry area away from water sources, he would have to bring along his own water or pay someone well to bring it for him. Cradling was less efficient than panning, but it allowed miners to process more dirt and usually resulted in more gold found at day's end.

EQUITED toil! Eureka! Look!
And read within those eyes
Their speaking luster, as they dwell
Upon the glittering prize!
The vein is struck! ah, noble heart!
A thrill of joy is thine!—
A purer and a better thrill
Than that produced by wine.
A thousand thoughts of home, and bliss
Reserved for coming years
Have swiftly flashed across thy soul
And melted thee to tears—
Tears—not of grief, or vain regrets,
For thou art still a man—
But, thinking of thy poverty
And gazing in the pan!

2

The Idle and Industrious Miner was published in Sacramento in 1854. Charles C. Nahl (1818–1878), a German-born artist, illustrated Alonzo Delano's morality tale, a type of story that was popular at the time and usually involved a conflict between right and wrong. *The Idle and Industrious Miner* was one of the projects on which the two men collaborated during their careers as artist and writer. Nahl was well-known for his artistic rendering of "forty-niners," as prospectors who had come west in the great migration of 1849 were often called. His sketches of nineteenth-century California life were often made into detailed woodcuts that appeared in books, newspapers, periodicals, and letter sheets during this time period.

amounts of soil than they could by panning. They invented the rocker, or cradle, an open trough set atop a base that could be rocked back and forth to "wash" larger amounts of dirt. Any gold would stick to wooden strips at the bottom of the cradle.

When dusk fell, the miners would return to their tents for dinner—usually pickled meat and coffee. When it got dark, there was little to do but go to bed or play poker and drink whiskey by the fire.

Soon, many of the small mining camps grew into busy towns. In particularly gold-rich districts, hundreds and sometimes thousands of argonauts would settle. Eager merchants settled there as well, ready to make their own fortune by supplying miners with items they needed, such as food, clothing, and tools. They also set up saloons and gambling halls to provide entertainment to the weary miners. The lifestyle took its toll on many who succumbed to their weaknesses for liquor and gambling.

Although reality usually proved them wrong, some miners believed that if they worked very hard and avoided the temptations of the mining towns, they would be rewarded for their clean living. This idea is conveyed on page 9 of *The Idle and Industrious Miner*. Shown on page 42 is the industrious miner, whose strong work ethic and virtuous ways lead him to his golden prize.

The life of a miner was another favorite topic for satire during the gold rush. There were definite codes of conduct miners were supposed to follow, regardless of whether they had a "virtuous" or "sinful" lifestyle. The letter sheet seen on page 44, *The Miners' Ten Commandments*, combined text and illustrations to poke fun at mining life and the "miner's code."

The first commandment was short and simple: "Thou shalt have no other claim than one." This was an actual rule found in many mining codes throughout the area at the time—a miner was allowed to work only one gold claim at a time. The eighth commandment was often considered the most difficult: "Thou shalt not steal a pick, or a shovel, or a pan, from thy fellow miner, nor take away his tools without his leave . . . for he will be sure to discover what thou hast done, and will straightway call his fellow miners together, and if the law hinder them not, they will hang thee, or give thee fifty lashes, or shave thy head and brand thee, like a horse thief, with R upon

The Miners' Ten Commandments by English-born author and editor James M. Hutchings was published in Placerville, California, by Sun Print in 1853. It is the best-known example of a satirical look at a miner's life. Miners found the letter sheet with its scenes representing life in the mines entertaining. Many people used it to decorate their tents or shacks. More than 100,000 copies were sold in just one year. The letter sheet was made from a wood engraving by Anthony & Baker, an engraving company in San Francisco.

thy cheek, to be known and read of all men, Californians in particular."

Though the letter sheet was satirical, such statements reflected real punishments for crimes that were committed among the miners.

The miners soon learned that the tales of gold nuggets the size of a man's fist were exaggerated, and many days, weeks, or months might pass before a miner found any gold at all. In the meantime, the miner would have to find another way to make a living. Men from the East who had been well respected and held well-paying jobs now found themselves doing whatever job they could find in exchange for lodging and food.

The life of riches the immigrants had envisioned rarely matched their real lives. Those prospectors who did manage to accumulate some wealth would often send money back home to their families. By doing so, they could earn their families pride and lessen the feelings of loneliness that sometimes seemed overwhelming. Companies began to spring up that allowed argonauts to transfer money safely from California to points throughout the country. Modern banking was beginning to take shape.

The 1850 receipt on page 46 states, "Received of T L Megquier Esq in apparent good order, to be transported in this Express Line, the undersigned articles, marked as per margin, which I promise to deliver in like good order, subject to the agreement now made and hereinafter expressed, to Carpenters Express at Boston."

In legal jargon, this means that Joseph W. Gregory's express service has received the indicated funds from Megquier—who is referred to here as "Esq," or esquire, a formal title commonly

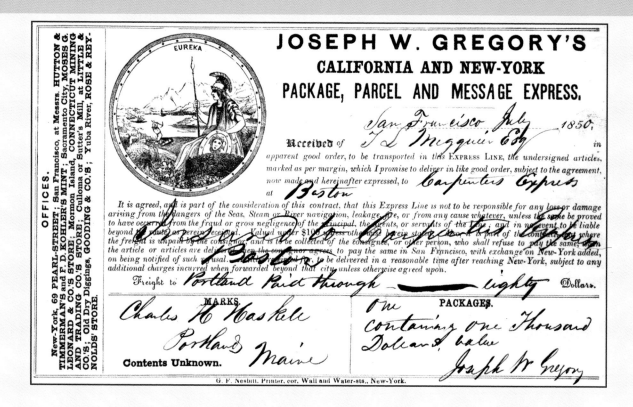

This receipt for Joseph W. Gregory's California and New-York Package, Parcel and Message Express service was filled out in July 1850. It is a record that Thomas L. Megquier transferred $1,000 from San Francisco, California, to a company called Carpenters Express in Boston, Massachusetts. Toward the bottom of the receipt, it is noted that "Freight to Portland Paid through eighty dollars," which means that Thomas Megquier paid $80 for the use of the express service between San Francisco and Portland, Maine. From Portland, Maine, the transfer to the final destination of Boston was likely carried out quickly, as the two cities are close by. Along the far left side is a listing of offices, likely indicating the facilities where Joseph W. Gregory's express service conducted operations. On the upper-left side of the receipt is the seal of California.

What eventually became California's state seal has changed a bit throughout the years, but this version is very similar to the one used today. The state seal, officially adopted in 1849, when California was still a territory, shows a grizzly bear next to the Roman goddess of wisdom, Minerva. The grizzly bear represents the republic of California, and it is also on the state's flag. In the background, a miner works with a pick, symbolizing the gold rush and the mining industry. Ships in the bay behind Minerva stand for California's trade, and the mountains represent the Sierra Nevada range. Wheat and grapes in the foreground represent California's agriculture.

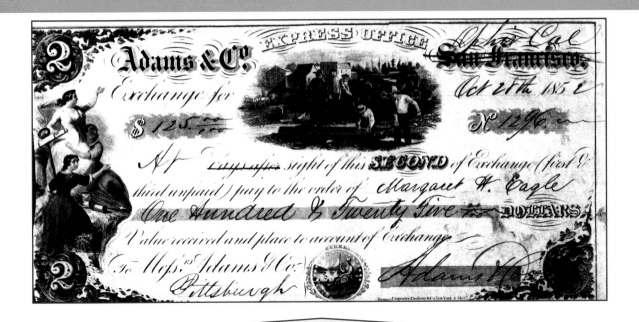

This receipt for Adams & Company express service was written out on October 28, 1852. It shows a record of $125 being transferred to Margaret H. Eagle in Pittsburgh, Pennsylvania, as indicated along the bottom left of the receipt. Although it is not noted on the receipt itself, the funds belonged to John Eagle. California's official seal appears at bottom center, and Adams's signature, seen in the lower-right corner, makes the paperwork for the transfer of funds official. A mining scene in the top middle of the receipt indicates that Adams & Company likely dealt primarily with fund transfers from miners in California to their families back East.

used at that time. Joseph W. Gregory is essentially promising that his company will deliver the funds safely, subject to the rules and regulations that are listed further down on the receipt. Joseph W. Gregory's signature in the lower-right corner (page 46) makes the agreement legally binding.

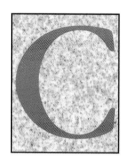

CHAPTER 6

THE LAWLESS WEST

Although many argonauts who had journeyed west to find gold had done so to improve their lives, difficult living conditions and greed motivated many to throw aside their principles and act in ways they would have never dreamed of before. The promise of instant wealth also attracted unscrupulous bandits who traveled around the region stealing what they liked from those who either couldn't defend themselves or found themselves outnumbered. The threat of violence was a constant presence in and around the mining camps, evident in the engraving seen on the facing page. A miner, represented in cartoon fashion, stands surrounded by four bandits. The miner carries an enormous pack on his back, labeled "Calafornia Gold," and towers above four rough-looking bandits who threaten him with huge knives, ready to murder him for his riches. Although the engraving is presented in an exaggerated style—with both the miner and his bag of treasure shown larger than life—its message is clearly based in the reality of the times. If a miner found gold, he might also find a knife at his throat.

This engraving entitled *Miner Is Accosted*, by an unknown artist, depicts the danger that abounded in the goldfields of California during the gold rush period. Although no date is available for the engraving, it was likely done sometime during the 1850s, when lawlessness was the rule rather than the exception in California's gold country.

Most of California's mining towns didn't have formal laws—just the "miner's code," rules that listed the miner's rights and responsibilities as a member of the mining community. There were no police to uphold the laws and no real jails to hold offenders. When laws were violated, other miners took justice into their own hands, often handing out harsh punishments. If a person was caught stealing, he might be branded so people would know his crime, or he might be publicly flogged. If a man was accused of murder, he didn't get a lawyer to defend him or have his case heard in front of a judge and jury. If a citizens' committee found him guilty, he could be publicly hanged. As a result, innocent men were sometimes killed for crimes they didn't commit, and the guilty often went free.

By 1850, California had enough people to be admitted to the United States as the thirty-first state. But as the population grew, so did the crime rate—without the luxury of time to develop a strong justice system to deal with offenders. Frustrated with the situation, a group of merchants came together in 1851 to form the Committee of Vigilance, thus taking matters out of the hands of elected government officials. The committee, which had about 700 members, set about preventing immigrants from disembarking at the city's docks, deporting people for crimes, and hanging accused murderers. The committee was dissolved within two months, only to re-form in 1856.

The grimness of life in California was a strong theme in much of the artwork and social commentary of the period. In the lithograph entitled *The Place We Hear About* (on page 52), violence breaks out as miners and thieves fight over gold.

Executive Committee Chamber
San Francisco September 5, 1856

John Stephens

Your written request to leave the State of California by the Steamer of this day has been received by the Executive Committee and I am directed to state to you that your prayer has been granted up-on the especial condition that you never return under the penalty of death.

By order of the Committee

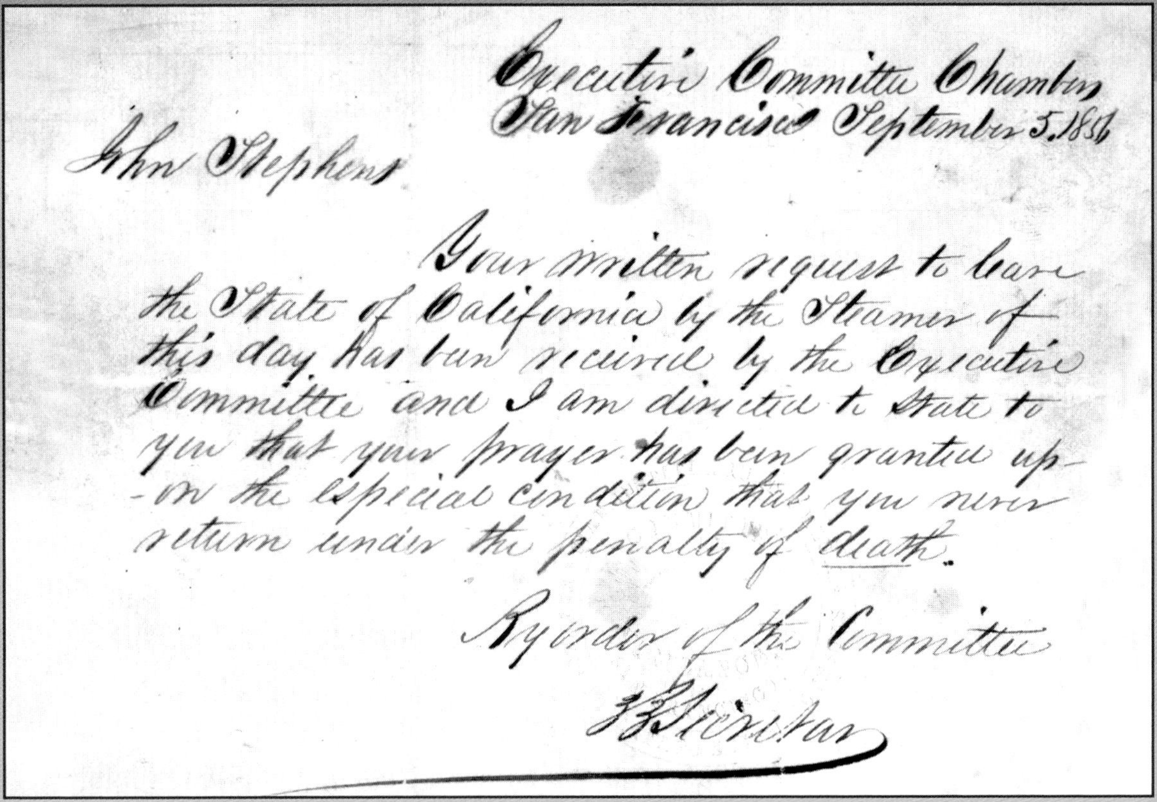

This letter, drafted by the 1856 vigilance committee, is typical of the kind of document they often used to achieve their political aims. The committee was run in a very organized manner, and those accused of crimes were given trials. Most of the committee's legal documents were written by a man named Isaac Bluxome Jr., who served as secretary of the organization's executive committee in 1851 and again in 1856. Bluxome signed the committee's documents with his serial number and office rather than his name, as seen here: "33 Secretary." This organized approach to legal dealings allowed the committee to maintain a profile of fairness as opposed to the alternative and prevalent form of justice—the lynch mob. In this letter, the man in question, John Stephens, has been granted his wish to leave San Francisco rather than be physically punished. The condition, however, is that he is never to return to California. If he does, he will be executed.

TRANSCRIPTION

Executive Committee Chamber
San Francisco September 5, 1856

John Stephens

Your written request to leave the State of California by the Steamer of this day has been received by the Executive Committee and I am directed to state to you that your prayer has been granted up-on the especial condition that you never return under the penalty of death.

By order of the Committee
33 Secretary

THE PLACE WE HEAR ABOUT.

It is believed that an artist named S. Lee Perkins drew this lithograph circa 1849. The lithograph was drawn on woven paper and measures 27.3 by 36.7 centimeters. It was published by Serrell & Perkins in New York City. The work bears a strong resemblance to Perkins's lithograph entitled *Things As They Are* in both its composition and style. A man in the center fires a gun at a miner who is carrying a large gold-filled sack. Men around them battle with their fists and knives. Illustrating the difficult living conditions and near starvation some experienced in the goldfields, one man demands another to give him food, exclaiming: "Bread! Bread! Damn you! Bread." On the right side, a man sits at a table, served by another man who demands, "A pinch of Gold for a drink." Nothing was without its price, including the most basic necessities like food and drink. On the left side we see a man kneeling and vomiting. Mountains rise up behind him, and several miners are shown diligently working their claim. No amount of turmoil, it seems, will take them from their task of finding gold.

In the background of *The Place We Hear About*, the Capitol building and the White House can be seen, as well as President James K. Polk and members of his cabinet, who carry pickaxes and shovels as they travel down the "High Road to California." Polk exclaims, "Off Boys to reap the reward of our four years labour." This was likely a direct jab at the political situation in the United States during the period. The United States had taken the territory of California from Mexico in February 1848 after winning the war it had been fighting with Mexico for nearly two years. This happened during Polk's presidency, and many viewed the president as a gold-hungry man more interested in gold than in the country's welfare. S. Lee Perkins, the artist, seems to agree.

Yet, it appears that Perkins was also fiercely patriotic when it came to the United States's right to California's gold, as seen in another lithograph he is thought to have done (see on page 54), entitled *The Defence of the California Bank*. In this political cartoon, the artist expresses the widely held opinion that California's treasures belonged to Americans and had to be kept safe from the greedy hands of foreign powers.

American distrust of foreign interests wasn't limited to leaders of other countries—it carried over to immigrant miners as well. California had become home to large numbers of Chinese, Australian, Mexican, and Latin American immigrants, to name just a few ethnic groups that came to California in search of gold and a better life. Americans from the East who had gone west for gold and settled in California were often racist and blamed California's problems on immigrants whose traditions and cultures they did not understand. Bigotry was a strong force, and many lynchings carried out during the gold rush were inflicted on innocent immigrants wrongly accused of crimes they didn't commit simply

The Defence of the California Bank was probably drawn by S. Lee Perkins and was published by Serrell & Perkins circa 1849 in New York City. Near the center, we see England's Queen Victoria, who approaches the shore riding a bull and carrying a shovel in her lap—clearly after California's gold. Behind her we see Russia's Czar Nicholas I, represented as a bear, an animal commonly associated with Russia. Overhead, France's newly elected president, Louis-Napoleon, is represented as a bird heading toward shore. Behind him is Queen Isabella of Spain, and behind her to the far right are American ships determined to defend the harbor against the foreign powers. On land we see future president Zachary Taylor as an eagle and President James K. Polk as a rattlesnake, symbolic of American power. American troops are shown on land, their camp composed of two rows of tents. Guards stand watch over crates of gold surrounding a flagpole that proudly flies the American flag. They will presumably guard America's riches to the death.

because their skin wasn't white. In 1850, a law was passed requiring foreign miners to pay twenty dollars a month for a mining permit. This law caused a lot of conflict between American and immigrant miners, and it was repealed the following year.

California's state legislature tried again in 1852, setting the foreign miners' tax at three dollars a month. This, coupled with the hostile discrimination and violence they faced each day, was enough to make many foreigners return to their home countries. Those who stayed often left the mining communities and cities so they might live in peace, finding work on rural farms instead. Native Americans and Californios (people of Mexican descent who had lived in California since it was a Mexican territory) sadly watched as California was corrupted by the eastern prospectors' greed.

Soon, the frenzied call of riches beyond a person's wildest dreams, which had beckoned hopeful argonauts from all over the world to the rolling hills of California, began to lose its luster. Some people's dreams had been realized and they had emerged with their golden prize, but most people's dreams had faded away, replaced with the realities of rough living and meager results. Within just a few years of James Marshall's discovery of gold, fewer and fewer people came to California, and those who did were far outnumbered by those who left. By the mid-1850s, many mining camps looked like ghost towns. Although the gold rush had happened just a few years earlier, people now told stories about what life had been like back then, when the lure of gold was all that mattered. To many, it had quickly become a distant memory.

But California's gold rush had left an indelible mark upon the land and had changed the face of the United States of America. It opened up the West and led to the first transcontinental railroad linking the East to California. New cities like San Francisco and Sacramento had sprung up and grown quickly, and western territories—like California—were admitted into the Union. Perhaps most important, many different people from many different cultures had become inextricably woven into the fabric of America.

PRIMARY SOURCE TRANSCRIPTIONS

Page 15: Lease Agreement

Transcription:

Gesn, Colule and Lole their heirs and assigns they paying the said Sutter and Marshall a reasonable price for the mill and buildings that may be put on the said premises by them.

In Witness whereof the said parties of the second [crossed out] first and second part set their names and seals, done this the fourth day of February in the year of our Lord one thousand eight hundred and fourty eight.

Witnesses	Pulpuli	his x chief mark	Seal
Charles Bennet,	Gesn	his x chief mark	Seal
William Scott.	Colule	his x alcalde mark	Seal
	Lole	his x alcalde mark	Seal
	J. A. Sutter,		Seal
	James W. Marshall.		Seal

Done in the presence and with my aprobation
J. A. Sutter—
[????] Indian Agent—

Contemporary English:

Gesn, Colule, and Lole and their heirs will pay Sutter and Marshall a reasonable price for the mill and buildings they may build on the land.

To show that they agree to this, Pulpuli, Gesn, Colule, Lole, Sutter, and Marshall have signed this and put their seals on it. This was done February 4, 1848.

This was done in my presence and with my approval.

Page 21: "Carriers' Address"

1.

Come on good friends—all other things give
    o'er,
We'll talk of Gold, on California's shore,
Gold! The great end and aim of human strife;
The all-exciting stimulus of life.
O, Power Supreme! man's earliest offerings
    shine
As votive gifts around thy glittering shrine.
Forever kneeling at thy altars proud,
Behold a suppliant, fawning, cringing crowd,
There offering up peace, honor, virtue, health,
To gain an entrance to the heaven of wealth.
Time was—time is—when gold's almighty sway
The high and low—the small and great obey.
It changes ill to good, and wrong to right;
Makes the disgusting fill us with delight.
The mean and groveling are, presto! made
Noble and generous, by its potent aid.
Tinged with its glare, the basest crimes
    assume
To mortal eyes the hue of virtue's bloom;
Changes the prate of fools to sayings good—
Makes dulness wit, not always understood!

2.

A beast that has it, with the gods is ranged,
A man without it to a beast is changed.
So by the almighty influence of gold
Fashion and morals both are thus controlled.
A line is drawn between the rich and poor,
Which no presumptuous mortal must pass o'er.
Give me but gold, you give me virtue,
    wisdom, grace,
Raise me at once to fashion's highest place;

And saints and sinners bow down and adore—
Not me in truth, but my rich glittering ore.
No wonder then the world is going mad—
No wonder then that thousand hearts
    are glad
To hear of regions in the far-off West,
With all untold, unthought-of treasures blest;
Where mother earth her golden treasures
    yields
Not to such toil as tills New England fields,
But places free before her outstretched hand
Her stores exhaustless of the glittering sand.

3.

Go then, ye slaves, to California's shore
Go delve and dig, and grasp the precious ore.
Leave home and friends, and all the heart
    holds dear,
There seek a comfort for each sorrow here,
Find all it needs, to make you rich and great,
To live in more than Dives' royal state,
To every want and every wish supply,
And then, poor delvers, give it up—and die!
While greedy heirs, expectant for your death,
With greedy eyes, shall watch your passing
    breath,
With outward woe, but inward joy profound,
Behold you safely nestled in the ground.
Well, you may die—your heirs possess your
    gains—
But still exhaustless from those distant plains,
With ceaseless flow, on rolls a golden tide
Till the most craving wishes are supplied;
Till, Midas-like, gold only meets our sight,
And sun and moon shine with a golden light.

GLOSSARY

amenity A feature that is considered pleasant or agreeable.

argonaut A name for gold rush-era miners in search of gold.

brand To mark by burning the skin with a hot iron.

cholera A disease usually characterized by severe distress in the stomach and intestines.

delirium A mental disturbance characterized by confusion, hallucinations, and disordered speech.

dysentery A disease usually caused by infection and characterized by severe diarrhea.

editorial A newspaper or magazine article that expresses the opinions of the publication's editors or publishers.

engraving An image made from a metal plate that has been carved into and then printed on a printing press.

forty-niner A person who went to California in search of gold in 1849.

gristmill A mill for grinding grain.

immigrant A person who comes to a country and takes up permanent residence.

isthmus A narrow strip of land that connects two larger pieces of land.

lease A contract by which one person or party passes land or real estate to another person or party, usually for a specified time period and for a specified rent.

lithograph A print that is made by printing from a flat surface, such as a metal plate.

malaria A disease caused by parasites in the red blood cells, usually transmitted by the bite of a mosquito and characterized by frequent attacks of fever and chills.

migration A movement from one place or country to another.

morality A system of virtues and rules of conduct.

prospector A person who explores an area, usually for mineral deposits like gold.

repeal To do away with something, as a law, by legally revoking it.

satire A literary device by which human vices, sin, and foolishness are pointed out and ridiculed.

telegraph A communication system in which coded signals are sent over an electric wire.

transcontinental Extending across a continent.

tributary A stream feeding a larger stream, river, or lake.

trough A long, shallow container.

vigilance committee A volunteer committee of citizens that comes together to punish criminals when the processes of law are incapable of doing so.

wagon train A line of wagons usually carrying supplies for a group of settlers who are traveling over land.

yellow fever A disease caused by a virus transmitted by the bite of a mosquito. Yellow fever is characterized by physical exhaustion, fever, protein in the urine indicating kidney disease, a yellowish cast to the skin, and often internal bleeding.

# FOR MORE INFORMATION

Web Sites

Due to the changing nature of Internet links, the Rosen Publishing Group, Inc., has developed an online list of Web sites related to the subject of this book. This site is updated regularly. Please use this link to access the list:

http://www.rosenlinks.com/psah/goru/

# FOR FURTHER READING

Altman, Linda Jacobs. *The California Gold Rush in American History*. Berkeley Heights, NJ: Enslow Publishers, Inc., 1997.

Blake, Arthur, and Pamela Dailey. *The Gold Rush of Eighteen Forty-Nine: Staking a Claim in California*. Brookfield, CT: Millbrook Press, Inc., 1995.

Hatch, Lynda. *The California Gold Rush Trail*. Parsippany, NJ: Good Apple, 1994.

Ito, Tom. *The California Gold Rush*. San Diego, CA: Lucent Books, 1996.

Schanzer, Rosalyn. *Gold Fever! Tales from the California Gold Rush*. Washington, DC: National Geographic Society, 1999.

Sherrow, Victoria. *Life During the Gold Rush*. San Diego, CA: Lucent Books, 1998.

Van Steenwyk, Elizabeth. *The California Gold Rush: West with the Forty-Niners*. Danbury, CT: Franklin Watts, Inc., 1991.

BIBLIOGRAPHY

Altman, Linda Jacobs. *The California Gold Rush in American History*. Berkeley Heights, NJ: Enslow Publishers, Inc., 1997.

Blodgett, Peter J. *Land of Golden Dreams: California in the Gold Rush Decade, 1848–1858*. San Marino, CA: Huntington Library Press, 1999.

California Historical Society. "The Gold Rush: California Transformed." 2000. Retrieved September 29, 2001 (http://www.californiahistory.net/goldFrame-2.htm).

California State Library. "California As We Saw It: Exploring the California Gold Rush." 2000. Retrieved September 25, 2001 (http://www.library.ca.gov/goldrush).

ComSpark. "Gold Rush Chronicles." 1998. Retrieved December 2, 2001 (http://www.comspark.com/chronicles).

Huntington Library. "Land of Golden Dreams: California in the Gold Rush Decade 1848–1858." 1999. Retrieved November 20, 2001 (http://www.huntington.org/Education/GoldRush).

Library of Congress. "California as I Saw It." 1998. Retrieved November 28, 2001 (http://memory.loc.gov/ammem/cbhtml/cbhome.html).

Museum of the City of San Francisco. "San Francisco Gold Rush." n.d. Retrieved November 30, 2001 (http://www.sfmuseum.org/hist1/index0.1.html#gold).

Oakland Museum of California. "California's Untold Stories: Gold Rush!" 1998. Retrieved December 10, 2001 (http://www.museumca.org/goldrush).

Sacramento Bee. "Gold Rush." n.d. Retrieved December 2, 2001 (http://www.calgoldrush.com).

Schanzer, Rosalyn. *Gold Fever! Tales from the California Gold Rush*. Washington, DC: National Geographic Society, 1999.

Van Steenwyk, Elizabeth. *The California Gold Rush: West with the Forty-Niners*. Danbury, CT: Franklin Watts, Inc., 1991.

INDEX

# PRIMARY SOURCE LIST

Page 9: Sketch drawn circa 1885 of gold site from James Wilson Marshall's cabin near Placerville, California. The sketch is now housed at the California State Library in Sacramento, California.

Page 12: *The Life and Adventures of James W. Marshall, The Discoverer of Gold in California*, a book published in 1870 by George Frederick Parsons. This is currently housed at the California State Library in Sacramento, California.

Page 14: Lithographed letter sheet of John Sutter's account of the gold rush, published in 1854 by publishers Britton & Rey. This is currently housed at the California State Library in Sacramento, California.

Page 15: Lease of 1848 signed by John Sutter and James Marshall, two chiefs (Pulpuli and Gesn), and two *alcaldes* (Colule and Lole) of the Yalisumni Indians. This is currently housed at the California State Library in Sacramento, California.

Page 19: Book by J. Ely Sherwood entitled *The Pocket Guide to California*, 1849. It is currently housed at the California State Library in Sacramento, California.

Page 21: Poem in the *Eastern Argus* called "Carriers' Address," printed in broadsheet form in 1849. This is currently housed at the California State Library in Sacramento, California.

Page 23: Lithograph produced in 1849 by Nathaniel Currier entitled *California Gold*. This is currently housed at the Library of Congress in Washington, D.C.

Page 25: *Persons from Nantucket*, a book published in 1850 by Jethro C. Brock. This is currently housed at the California State Library in Sacramento, California.

Page 27: Map of water routes to California, published in 1849 by Ensign & Thayer. This is currently housed at the California State Library in Sacramento, California.

Page 30: Advertisement for the sail of the ship *Balance* to Sacramento, California, on December 26, 1848. This is currently housed at the California State Library in Sacramento, California.

Page 31: Daguerreotype, date unknown, of Reverend Joseph A. Benton by an unknown artist. This is currently housed at the California State Library in Sacramento, California.

Page 32: Diary from 1849 of Reverend Joseph A. Benton. This is currently housed at the California State Library in Sacramento, California.

Page 33: Hand-colored lithograph of San Francisco by William Birch McMurtrie in 1851. This is currently housed at the California State Library in Sacramento, California.

Page 35: Letter sheet of *Hutchings' Panoramic Scenes—Crossing the Plains,* circa 1854, by James M. Hutchings. This is currently housed at the California State Library in Sacramento, California.

Page 39: Lithograph by Henry R. Robinson, published circa 1850. This is currently housed at the California State Library in Sacramento, California.

Page 41: Woodcut of gold miners by an unknown artist from 1854.

Page 42: *The Idle and Industrious Miner*, illustrated and written by Charles C. Nahl and Alonzo Delano, 1854.

Page 44: *The Miners' Ten Commandments*, circa 1853, by James M. Hutchings. This is currently housed at the Library of Congress in Washington, D.C.

Page 46: Receipt for Thomas L. Megquier's transfer of $1,000, 1850. This is currently housed at the Huntington Library in San Marino, California.

Page 47: Receipt for Adams & Company express service for a transfer of $125, 1852. This is currently housed at the Huntington Library in San Marino, California.

Page 49: Engraving of lawlessness in goldfields of California called *Miner Is Accosted* by unknown artist circa 1850.

Page 51: Letter by vigilance committee, 1856, by Isaac Bluxome Jr. This is currently housed at the Library of Congres in Washington, D.C.

Page 52: Lithograph titled *The Place We Hear About*, circa 1849, published by Serrell & Perkins in New York City. The artist is believed to be S. Lee Perkins. It is currently housed at the Library of Congress in Washington, D.C.

Page 54: *The Defence of the California Bank*, published by Serrell & Perkins circa 1849. This is currently housed at the Huntington Library in San Marino, California.

About the Author

Kerri O'Donnell received her degree in journalism from New York University. She is a writer and editor currently residing in Buffalo, New York.

Photo Credits

Cover, p. 1 © Hulton/Archive/Getty Images; pp. 9, 12, 14, 15, 21, 23, 25, 27, 30, 31, 32, 33, 35, 39 © California State Library; pp. 19, 44, 51, 52 © Library of Congress; pp. 41, 49 © Corbis; pp. 42, 46, 47, 54 © Huntington Library.

Editor

Annie Sommers

Design

Nelson Sá